Mel Bay Presen

# LEARN
# TO
# BURN
## on Rock Guitar

### By Vince Lauria

STEREO CASSETTE TAPE AVAILABLE

# Foreword

The intention of the first section of this book is to share with you, the student, the most commonly used patterns and devices used in rock guitar playing. I have not gone into the theoretical explanations of the materials presented. In my years of teaching I have found it better to start playing the sounds you like so that your interest and enthusiasm are maintained. Many times, when students begin lessons by reading and studying basic chords for months at a time, their desire to play is lessened greatly. My hope is that, by giving materials that strengthen and encourage your own creativity, you are more likely to stay with the guitar, enjoy it more, and play just for fun. Then your desire to read music, understand musical theory and more in-depth musical concepts will naturally develop. So hang in there, and keep playing and having fun.

# Dedication

This book is dedicated to all lovers of burning rock guitar and to these people who have contributed to my love and abilities on guitar:

| | | |
|---|---|---|
| Chris Ayres | Dan & Dee Ferguson | Steve Small |
| John Cosgrove | Kay Guerin | Danny Loi |
| Jimi Hendrix | Tommy Tedesco | Chad Thompson |
| Eric Clapton | John & Brenda Roberts | Bill Stewart |
| Ira Ingber | Jim & Lori Hansen | Jeff Malham |
| Christopher Parkening | Rafael Garcia | Mike Ringrose |

and to the memory of my parents, Aggidio and Charolene Lauria, and to my family Gary, Gail, Gigg, and Renee'. Special thanks to Murray K. Jacob and Bill Rosen.

# Credits

## FORMER STUDENTS

Jimmy McNichols—Television Recording Star
Dave Marks, Beach Boys—Recording Star

## TELEVISION AND RECORDING PROJECTS

Leon Russell Cable Video Show
Made In The Shade Jeans Commercial
Walt Disney Movie "The Tiger and The Rock Star"
Grinding Machine Project

Vince has studied and played guitar for over 15 years. This includes, but is not limited to, classical, jazz, and rock techniques and conducting group workshops and private instruction.

# Table of Contents

# Vince's Comments

This book is made for the person who is tired of going through the jungle of boring, slow-advancing guitar lessons. Through my years of listening, playing, and teaching, I have used many methods. The ones that have gained the greatest and quickest results are presented in this book. This book is designed so that a beginner or intermediate student will gain the greatest results within the shortest amount of time to make anyone a great rock guitar player. No one book tells it all, but if you use any part of this book you will at least triple your abilities on the guitar. Use the book in the sequence given to acquire maximum abilities for the time used. Always start slowly and clearly and gradually build speed for best results. Practice, not luck, pays off! Have fun and enjoy.

---

**To play rock guitar, three things are required:**

**A. Listen closely to your favorite players and composers.**
**B. Work a set daily practice routine.**
**C. "Jam," practicing at least once or more a week with a friend, drummer, guitarist, bassist, drum machine, or drum drops (prerecorded drummer on tape).**

---

These three things together create maximum growth. This book is designed to provide the building blocks that are 1,000% necessary to playing rock guitar like a pro. In the next section, I will explain the tablature that is used throughout the first section of this book. Make sure you understand that before proceeding with this book.

# Neck and Hand Diagrams

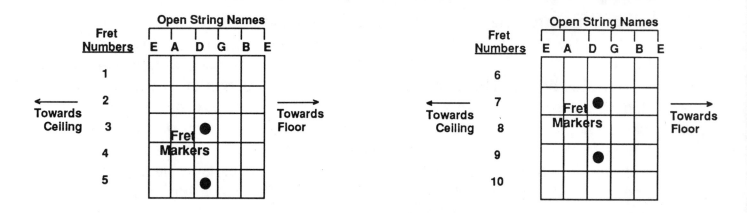

1) **Memorize open string names E A D G B E.**
2) **Memorize markers in relation to fret number positions—3, 5, 7, 9, 12, 15, 17, 19, 21. (This makes it easy to find any fret quickly without counting up the neck each time.)**

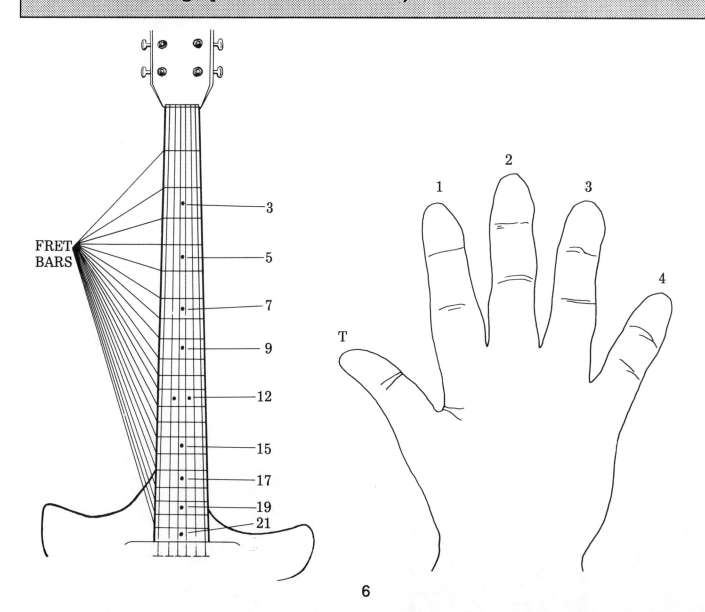

# Tablature

This shorthand is used throughout the book. Refer to this page when needed.

| | |
|---|---|
| **B** | = Bend (to bend the string to desired tone) |
| **H** | = Hold (to hold a note while picking next note) |
| **HO** | = Hammer-on (to use finger strength alone to tap on fret from one note to another) |
| **HU** | = Hold up (to hold up a note usually to pick another note) |
| **LD** | = Let down (to let down the note you were holding up) |
| **P** | = Pick (to pick string) |
| **PO** | = Pull-off (to use finger strength to pull off from a note to another note) |
| **R** | = Root or key note |
| **S** | = Slide (to move along frets) |
| **TR** | = Trill (HO + PO in succession) |
| **V** | = Vibrato (to move finger back and forth on fret) |

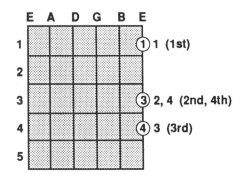

The number inside a circle indicates which finger to use and the string and fret on which to place it.

The number outside a circle indicates the order in which to play that finger. Sometimes the same finger is used more than once per diagram.

# Exercise Schedule

When holding the pick, hold it at a 45° angle toward the floor. This helps you to play clearer and faster. I recommend extra-heavy guitar picks for modern-day rock guitar sound.

The next pages of exercises are designed to be played slowly at first. Remember to keep left-hand fingers on tips and arched. Keep left-hand thumb on lower middle to middle of back of guitar neck. These exercises must be done as close to time shown as possible for maximum results. Remember to use down/up picking on all diagrams— one note down, one note up. ALWAYS START DOWN!

## FIRST WEEK
Five to fifteen minutes on finger exercises.
Ten to twenty minutes on scale forms.
Five to fifteen minutes on rock rhythm exercises.

## SECOND WEEK
Twenty to thirty minutes on finger exercises.
Twenty to thirty minutes on scale forms.
Twenty to thirty minutes on rock rhythm exercises.
Record thirty minutes of chord progressions,
then play scale and riffs live to tape.

## FOURTH TO EIGHTH WEEKS
Thirty to forty minutes on finger exercises.
Thirty to forty minutes on scale forms.
Thirty to forty minutes on rock rhythm exercises.
Record forty minutes of chord progressions,
then play scale and riffs live to tape.

Remember it's better to do five minutes a day of everything than nothing at all. The first six months on the guitar are the toughest. If you hang on that long, you can go all the way to being a great rock guitar player.

# Finger Exercises

All diagrams should be played from left to right.

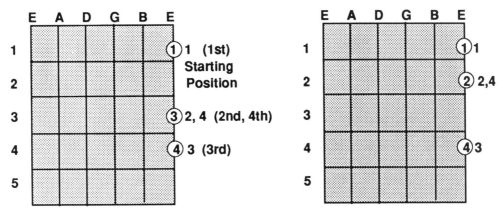

Repeat exercise ten times on each string. Do all six strings.

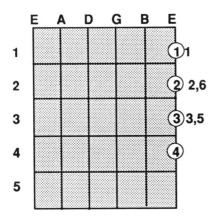

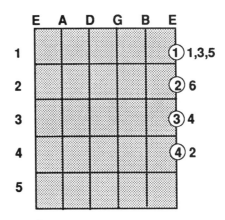

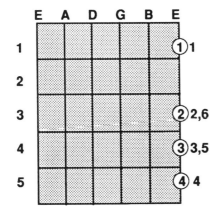

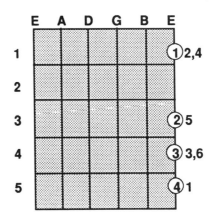

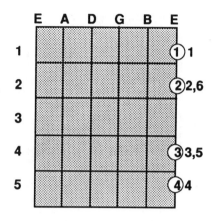

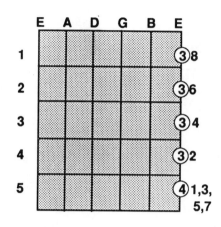

Use the minimum amount of finger movement.  Keep fingers as close to fret board as possible.

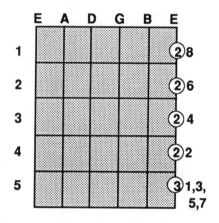

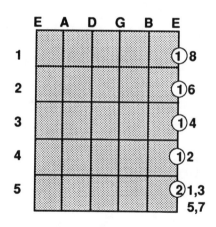

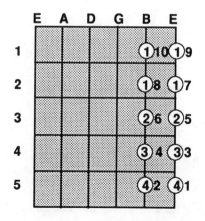

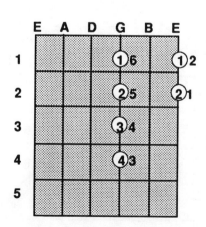

# Rock Rhythm Chord Exercises

When learning rock guitar, it is important to know commonly used rhythm patterns. The next exercises I will give are used in 90% to 100% of all rock songs you will encounter. Again, remember to refer to the numbers next to the fingers for the order used. Now refer to the diagram:

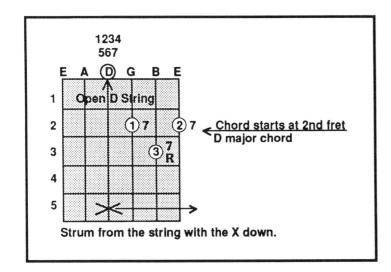

Remember to slide fingers to next frets. Also try to slide to next fret position while picking open D string.

Place fingers on proper string for D major chord. Now pick open D string alone six times. On seventh time, pick open D string and strum D chord down at same time. Now repeat whole idea until it's comfortable, then do 4th fret, then 5, 7, 9, 7, 5, 4, 2 frets. Then do the following fret combinations. Remember, first finger shows which fret chord is started. This applies to all chords.

## Chord Progressions

| D Blues Scale Forms (See pp. 17, 27, 28, 44, 45) |
|---|
| 1. (2, 5, 7, 2) x 50 |
| 2. (5, 7, 9, 4, 2) x 50 |
| 3. (9, 4, 5, 2) x 50 |
| 4. (4, 5, 4, 9) x 50 |

Transpose G blues to D blues and play with progressions.

| D Major, D Pentatonic Scale Forms (See pp. 15, 16, 27, 28, 44,45) |
|---|
| 5. (2, 7, 9) x 50 |
| 6. (2, 9, 7, 9) x 50 |
| 7. (2, 7, 9, 14) x 50 |
| 8. (9, 2, 7, 2, 5) x 50 |

Transpose G major to D major and play with progressions.

Now do the same idea as before with D major, except with the B♭ chord on these frets:  1, 3, 5, 7, 8, 10, 8, 7, 5, 3, 1.

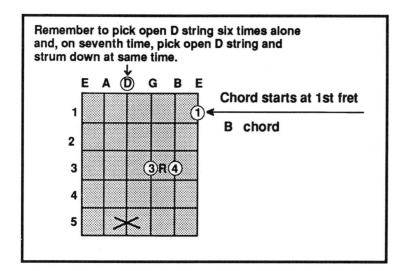

Remember to pick open D string six times alone and, on seventh time, pick open D string and strum down at same time.

Chord starts at 1st fret

B♭ chord

Now try these fret combinations:

| **D Blues Scale Forms** |
| (See pp. 17, 27, 28, 44, 45) |
| 1. (1, 5, 3, 5) x 50 |
| 2. (10, 5, 1, 5) x 50 |
| 3. (3, 5, 1, 10) x 50 |

Now do the same idea with the F chord.

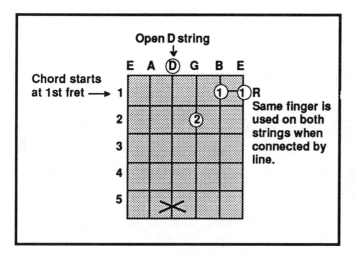

Open D string

Chord starts at 1st fret

R

Same finger is used on both strings when connected by line.

Now try these fret combinations:

| **D Major, D Pentatonic Scale Forms** |
| (See pp. 15, 16, 27, 28, 44, 45) |
| 1. (10, 3, 5, 3) x 50 |
| 2. (10, 5, 3, 5) x 50 |
| 3. (10, 3, 10, 5) x 50 |

Now we will combine all three chords for thousand of possibilities. Using the same strumming pattern as before, combine as given below. Remember to pick open D string six times. On seventh time, strum down open D string and chord.

<table>
<tr><td colspan="12" align="center">**D Blues Scale Forms**<br>(See pp. 17, 27, 28, 44, 45)</td></tr>
<tr><td>Fret No.</td><td>2</td><td>4</td><td>5</td><td>3</td><td>1</td><td>1</td><td>2</td><td></td><td></td><td></td><td></td></tr>
<tr><td>Chord</td><td>D</td><td>D</td><td>D</td><td>B♭</td><td>B♭</td><td>F</td><td>D</td><td>x 50</td><td></td><td></td><td></td></tr>
<tr><td>Fret No.</td><td>1</td><td>3</td><td>5</td><td>3</td><td>5</td><td>7</td><td>8</td><td>5</td><td>4</td><td>5</td><td></td></tr>
<tr><td>Chord</td><td>B♭</td><td>B♭</td><td>B♭</td><td>B♭</td><td>D</td><td>D</td><td>F</td><td>D</td><td>D</td><td>B♭</td><td>x 50</td></tr>
<tr><td>Fret No.</td><td>3</td><td>1</td><td>1</td><td>5</td><td>2</td><td></td><td></td><td></td><td></td><td></td><td></td></tr>
<tr><td>Chord</td><td>F</td><td>F</td><td>B♭</td><td>D</td><td>D</td><td>x 50</td><td></td><td></td><td></td><td></td><td></td></tr>
<tr><td>Fret No.</td><td>5</td><td>5</td><td>3</td><td>3</td><td>1</td><td>1</td><td>2</td><td></td><td></td><td></td><td></td></tr>
<tr><td>Chord</td><td>B♭</td><td>F</td><td>B♭</td><td>F</td><td>B♭</td><td>F</td><td>D</td><td>x 50</td><td></td><td></td><td></td></tr>
</table>

Same idea as before, except on a different string set. Use first finger to cover the D, G, and B strings. (This makes it easier to strum D and G strings without having to arch finger.) Pick open A string alone six times. On seventh time, strum down open A string and chord together. For C major, C pentatonic scale forms, see pp. 15, 16, 27, 28, 44, 45.

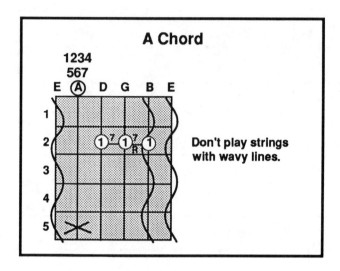

Now slide first finger to these frets doing the same chord idea: 2, 4, 5, 7, 9, 10, 9, 7, 5, 4, 2. Create your own fret combinations.

Same idea as before, except do these frets: 3, 5, 7, 9, 10, 12, 10, 9, 7, 5, 3, 2.

Create your own fret combinations. For G major, G pentatonic scale forms, see pp. 15, 16, 27, 28, 44, 45.

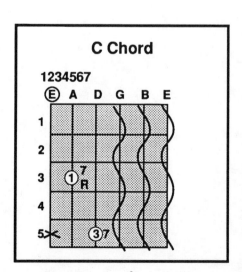

# Movable Major Scale Forms

The diagrams below are in G major. 99% of all music in the world, including rock songs and solos, is derived from the notes in the major scale. By knowing these scale forms *before* learning any leads, you will be able to quickly see and understand where all leads in songs are derived. Some famous people who have utilized these forms are Randy Rhoads, Jimi Hendrix, and Eddie Van Halen. You can see they are used by the best. So memorize the forms below starting from the lowest tone note in the scale form. Do each finger on each string, then progress up in tone to the next closest string. Refer to number order outside finger if necessary. Do the same thing with the blues and pentatonic scale forms, as these are used very often in rock and roll playing. All examples are given in the key of G even though they start at different frets.

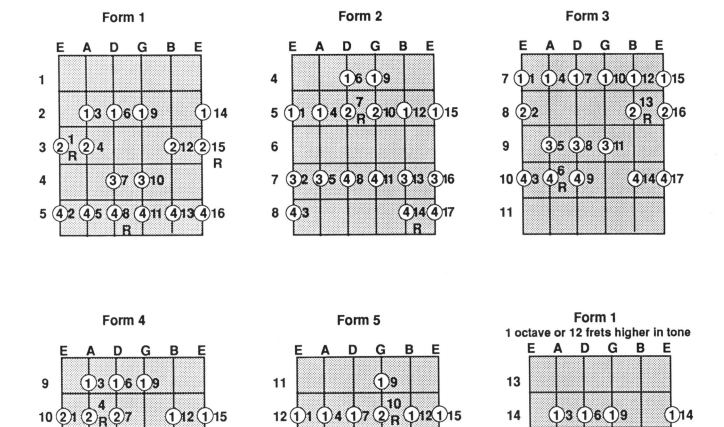

To transpose scale forms to all 12 keys, see pp. 27 and 28.

15

# Movable Pentatonic Scale Forms

These are movable to all 12 keys.  All forms are in the key of G.

**Form 1**

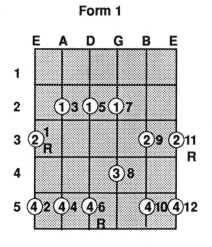

**Form 2**

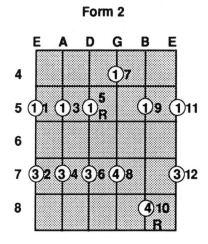

**Form 3**

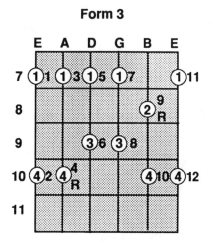

**Form 4**

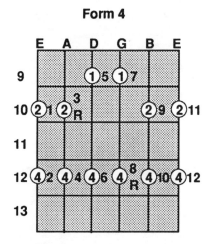

**Form 5**

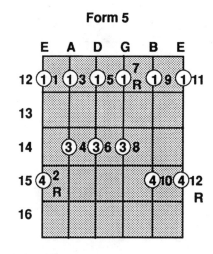

**Form 1**
1 octave higher in tone

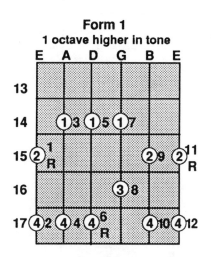

# Movable Blues Rock Scale Forms

All forms are in the key of G.

### Form 1
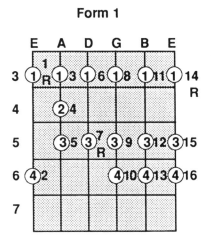

### Form 2
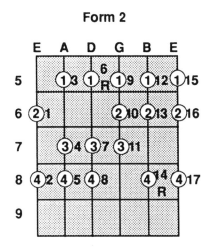

### Form 3
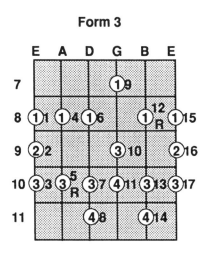

### Form 4
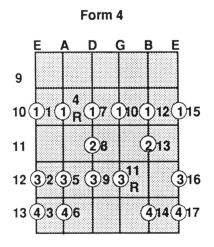

### Form 5
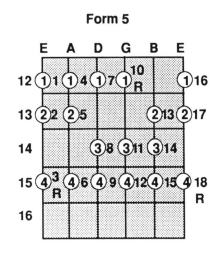

### Form 1
**one octave higher in tone**
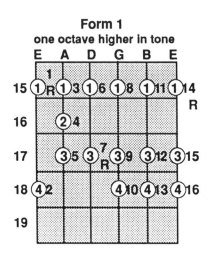

17

# G Blues Progression

These progressions are to be used in relation to riffs on pp. 21-26. By learning the blues chord progression, you will be able to get a good feel for rock and roll. Blues is the foundation for rock guitar, and it is the universal chord progression which will enable you to develop your own style and help you when jamming with other musicians.

There are many ways you can play standard blues. My three favorite ways are on the next page. Learn one at a time, memorize it, and then record it or have a friend play rhythm guitar while you play G blues riffs. Then let *him* solo while *you* play rhythm. Always practice rhythm guitar with a metronome or some other even beat, like a drum machine, drum drops, or a live drummer. Remember that rhythm guitar playing *is* important. The best players are *always* excellent rhythm players. If your rhythm is weak, your leads will lack *tightness* and *punch*.

In the following example, the three main chords in G blues are G, C, and D. Notice that the same riff is used in the same three keys.

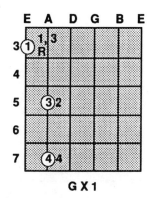

G X 1

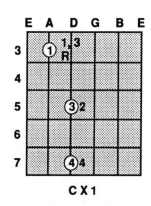

C X 1

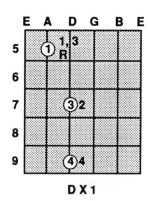

D X 1

18

## Version 1

X 50 (GX2, CX2, GX4, CX4, GX4, DX2, CX2, GX2)
Turn-Around Riff

## Version 2

X 50 (GX4, CX2, GX4, DX2, CX2, GX2)
Turn-Around Riff

## Version 3

X 50 (GX8, CX4, GX4, DX4, GX2)
Turn-Around Riff

The number after the letter indicates how many times to play that riff. The turn-around riff is used every time at the end of the blues progression; it starts the entire blues progression over again. This one turn-around riff is used for all three versions above:

## Turn-Around Riff

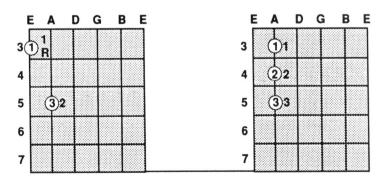

# Most Commonly Used Riffs

In addition to rock rhythm playing, I will now diagram rock's most commonly used riff patterns. Refer to tablature to understand how to play these. Once you have learned these riffs as I have given them, you will then be able to create your own lead riff combinations by experimentation. This, combined with the rock rhythms previously learned, will give you a good foundation for the techniques that are used in the majority of rock songs. You will, by experimentation, be able to recognize and learn quickly most heavy rock songs and riffs and lead solos. Remember, before playing *each* riff, always *check* the following:

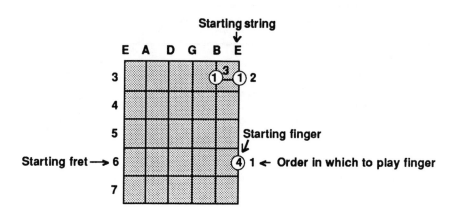

Examples are given in the key of G, but these can be used for all 12 keys. Do each diagram at least 50 times a day.

# Most Commonly Used Rock Riffs
### Off Blues Rock Form 1, pg. 17

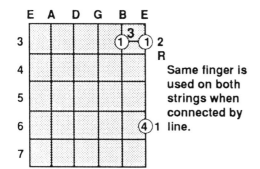

Same finger is used on both strings when connected by line.

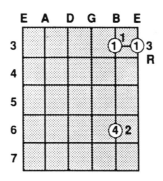

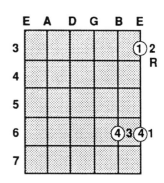

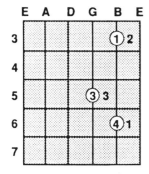

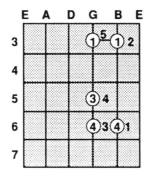

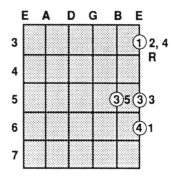

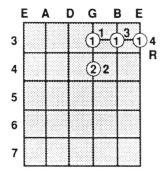

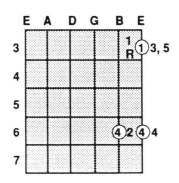

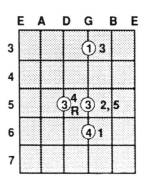

21

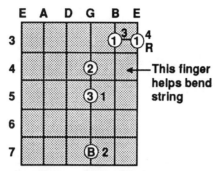

P1 B to 2 HU2 P3 P4 LD2
This means pick 1 and bend up to the note
(if you were playing 2). Then, holding up
the bend, pick 3, 4, then let down 2.

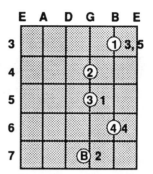

P1 B to 2 HU2 P3 LD2 P4 P5

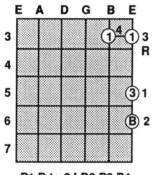

P1 B to 2 LD2 P3 P4

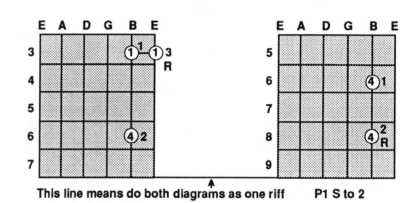

This line means do both diagrams as one riff          P1 S to 2

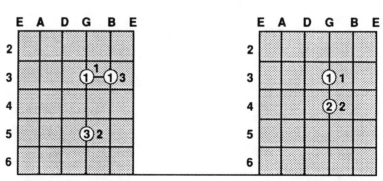

P1 B to 2 HU2 P3 LD to 4

P1 HO to 2

**When the same number is by two different strings, play both strings at the same time**

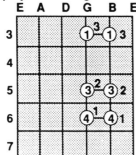

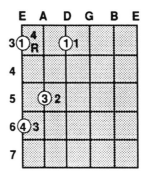

## Blues Rock Form 2

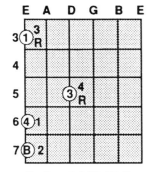

P1 B to 2 LD2 P3 P4

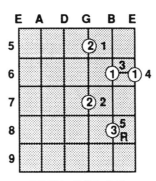

P1 S to 2 P3, 4, 5

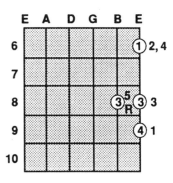

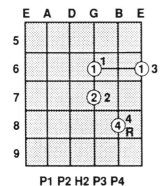

P1 P2 H2 P3 P4

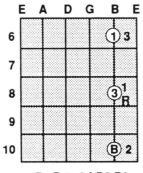

P1 B to 2 LD2 P3

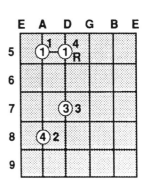

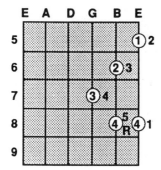

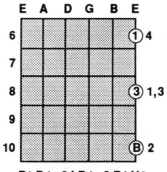

**P1 B to 2 LD to 3 P4 V4**

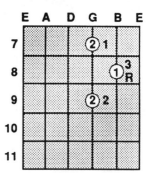

**P1 S to 2 P3**

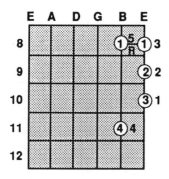

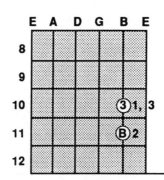

**P1 B to 2 LD to 3**

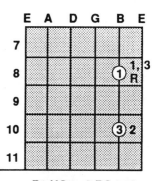

**P1 HO to 2 PO to 3**

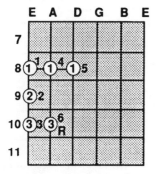

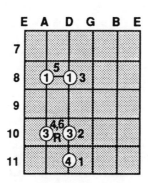

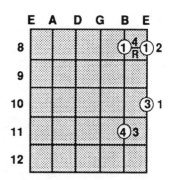

## Blues Rock Form 4

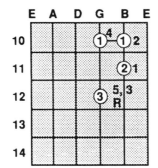

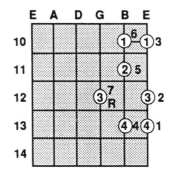

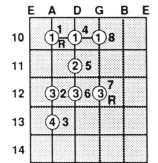

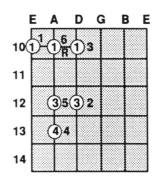

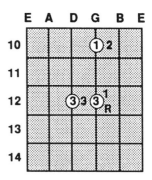

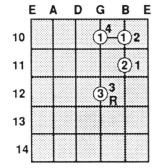

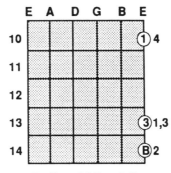

P1 B to 2 LD to 3 P4

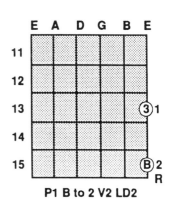

P1 B to 2 V2 LD2

25

## Blues Rock Form 5

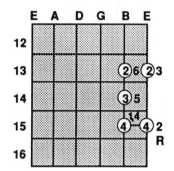

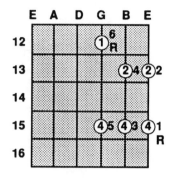

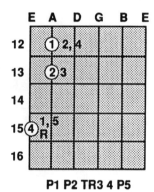

P1 P2 TR3 4 P5

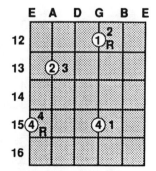

P1 B to 2 V2 LD2

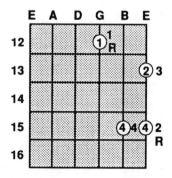

# Transposition

To transpose simply means to move to another key. The root note in a scale or chord is the note that the scale or chord is started on. All scales and chords have an "R" next to the root note. By using the note name chart on pg. 47, start at the root note you are on and then go to the desired root note by moving your hand up or down the neck. For example, to change G blues (scale form 1) to D blues (scale form 1), slide your hand starting with the 3rd fret to the 10th fret. (See example below.) Transpose forms 1 through 5 to D blues. Refer to pg. 17.

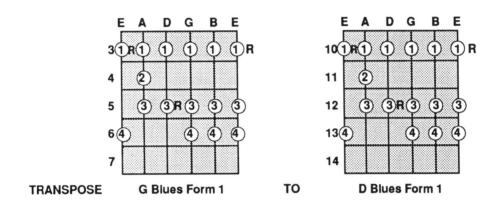

TRANSPOSE    G Blues Form 1    TO    D Blues Form 1

To transpose G major (form 1) to D major (form 1), just slide your hand starting with the 3rd fret to the 10th fret. This rule applies to all forms 1 through 5. Start with form 1 first and then forms 2, 3, 4, 5. Remember to refer to note name chart on pg. 47 to find all the note names on all of the strings and fret positions. Transpose forms 1 through 5 to D major. Refer to pg. 15.

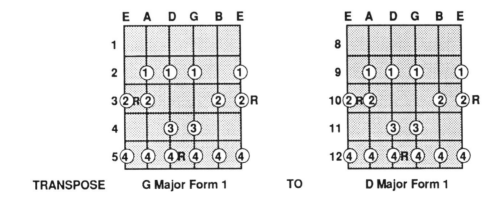

TRANSPOSE    G Major Form 1    TO    D Major Form 1

This same idea applies to chords.  To transpose a D major chord to an E major chord, just slide your hand from the 2nd fret to the 4th fret.  (See examples below.)

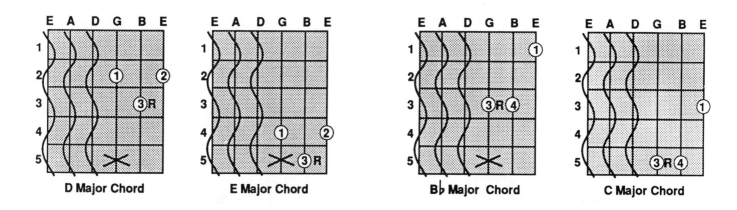

| D Major Chord | E Major Chord | B♭ Major Chord | C Major Chord |

Now you can transpose the following to their new keys:  D chord to F chord; B♭ chord to D chord; F chord to A chord.  Also transpose the following scale forms:  G blues to E blues; G major to A major; G pentatonic to B♭ pentatonic.  Transpose all chords and scale forms to a new key once a week using any of the 12 keys you like. (Refer to note name chart on pg. 47.)

# D Major Scale Riffs

## Major Rock Form 1

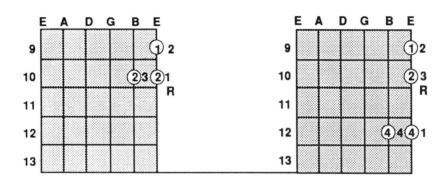

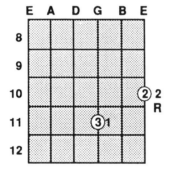

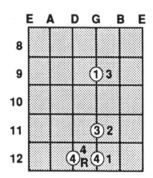

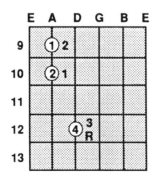

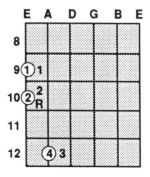

# Form 2

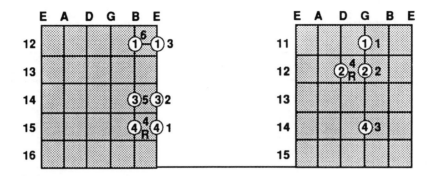

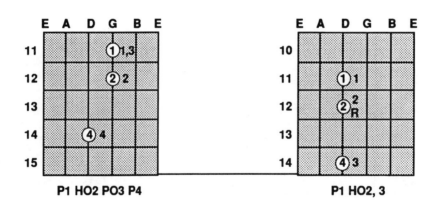

P1 HO2 PO3 P4                    P1 HO2, 3

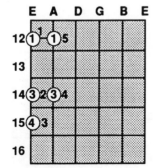          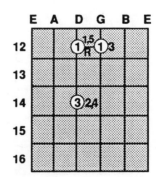

# Form 3

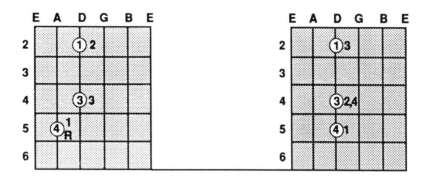

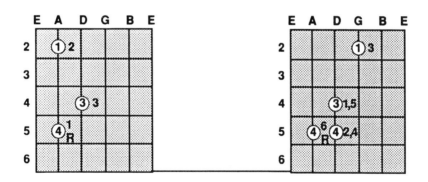

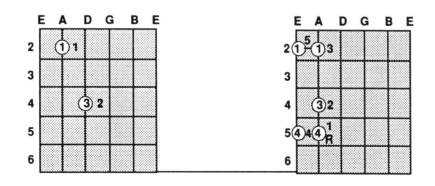

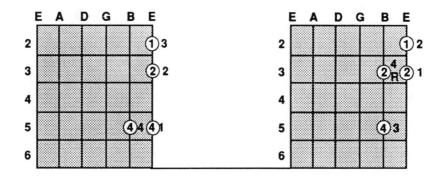

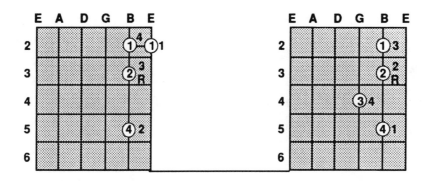

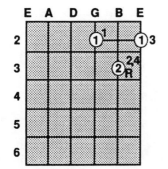

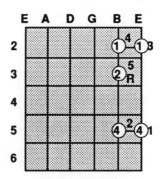

# Form 4

Form 4

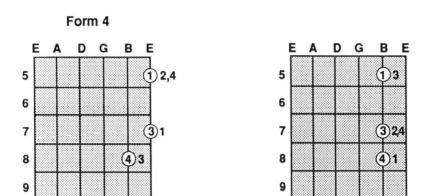

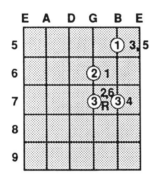

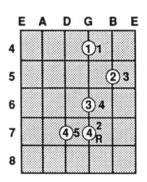

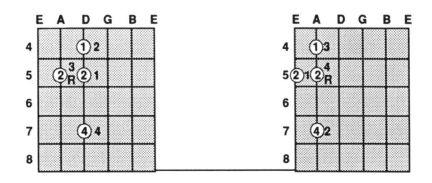

# Form 5

Form 5

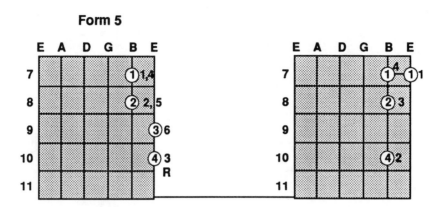

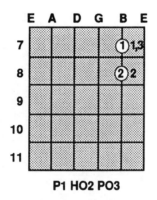

P1 HO2 PO3

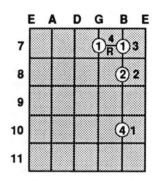

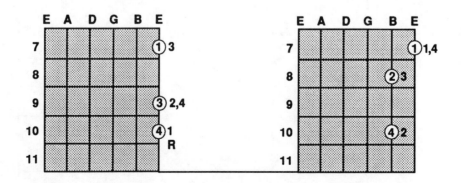

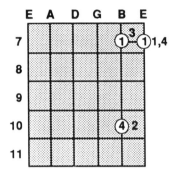

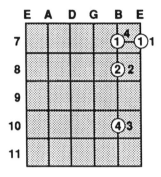

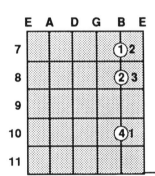

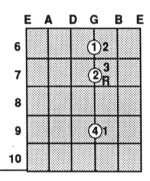

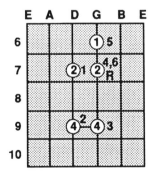

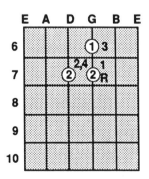

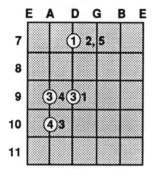

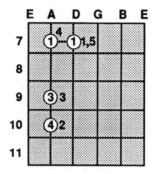

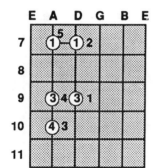

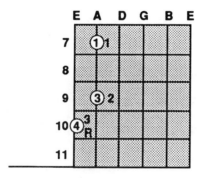

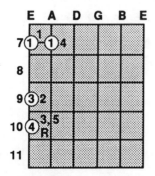

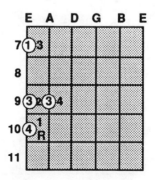

# D Pentatonic Scale Riffs

## Form 1

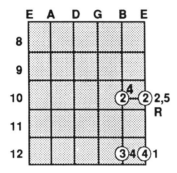

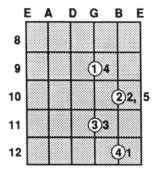

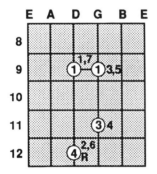

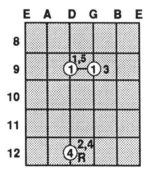

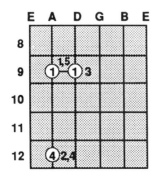

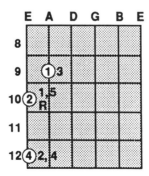

# Form 2

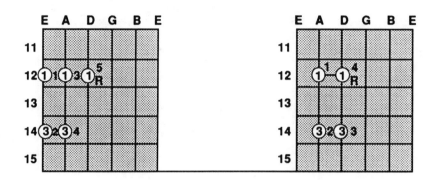

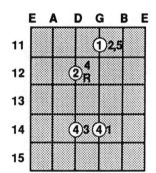

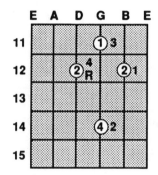

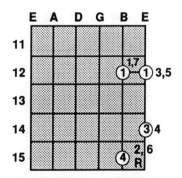

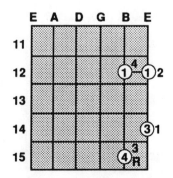

# Form 3

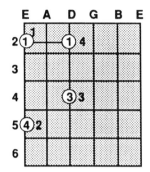

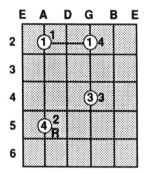

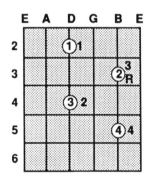

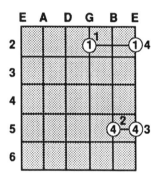

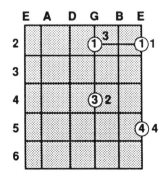

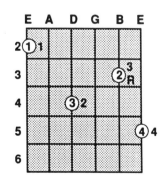

# Form 4

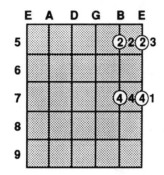

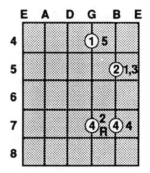

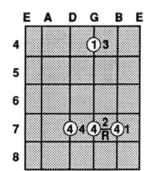

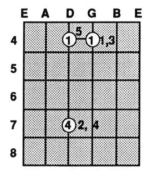

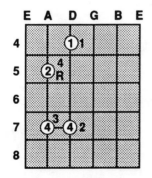

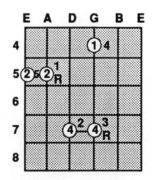

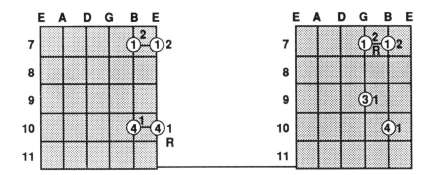

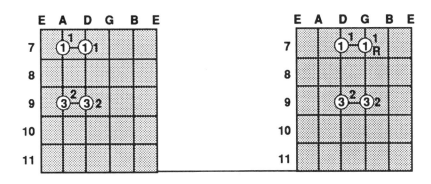

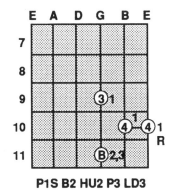

**P1S B2 HU2 P3 LD3**

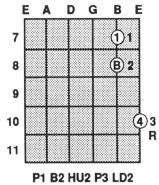

**P1 B2 HU2 P3 LD2**

43

# Tips for Riffs

When playing riffs, always take one riff at a time and play it until it becomes natural. When the chords are played for that type of riff (major, pentatonic, or blues), concentrate on the riff so it will sound smooth and musical.

Remember at first: Always start chords and riffs slowly. I can't say this enough because, when they are played fast at first, it always leads to frustration, confusion, and then boredom. REMEMBER! Start slowly and make the riffs and chords sound smooth and musical. Fewer notes played slowly and properly will develop your musical abilities faster, and speed will develop in time. Force yourself to play slowly and accurately—gradually building your speed with a metronome or drum machine. When you have three or more riffs from the same scale memorized, then experiment with them by combining them in different orders—one right after the other—in a continuous flow.

Always use even eighth notes when playing scale forms. Eighth notes are counted "one and two and three and four and." They are the down and up accents of four beats. REMEMBER: Always pick down/up—down/up as this makes the riffs sound much more fluid and will help develop your right- and left-hand coordination.

When creating your own riffs off scale forms, start with only four notes—then listen to what you are playing. Use your hands and ears together so you hear the melody. The melody is the arrangement of single notes in succession together with rhythm. Now you can bend, hammer on, pull off, and slide—which will only add to the fullness of those original notes. You will be able to create as many riff ideas as you want. RE-MEMBER to use only those *four notes* for at least 15 minutes at a time. This exercise will give you the ability to develop your own style.

When bending strings, always bend the G, B, and E strings toward the ceiling. When bending the E, A, and D strings, always bend towards the floor.

Now, when you have learned all the riffs given in this book, refer to the note name chart on pg. 47 and learn each riff in three octaves on the neck. (See example below.) By using this technique, you will triple the number of riffs in this book.

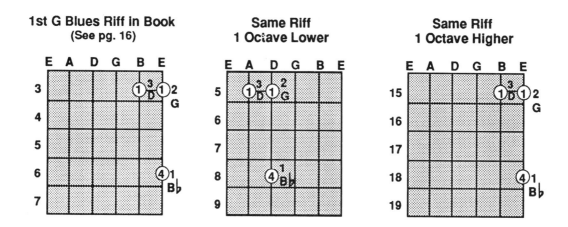

# Most Commonly Used Chords

Transpose these chords to all 12 keys (refer to pp. 27 and 28). These chords are given in the key of C. Strum from the string with the X down.

### C Major

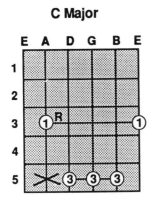

### C Minor

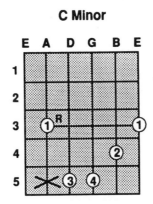

### C Major 7th

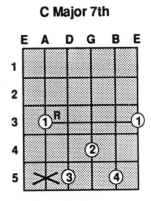

### C Minor 7th

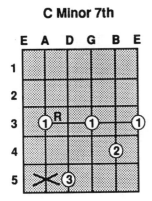

### C Dominant 7th

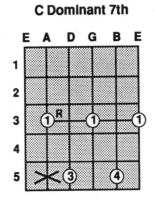

### C Minor Add 9th

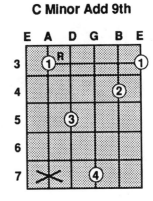

### C 11

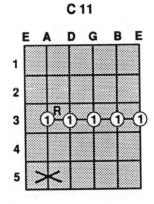

### C 13th

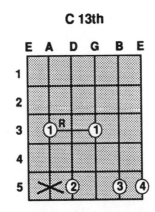

### C 9th

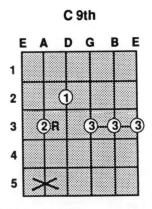

# String Note Name Chart

To help you, here is a chart with the string and note names that match with their positions on the neck. Our musical system uses 12 notes. Seven names we take from the alphabet (ABCDEFG). The other five notes are a combination of letter names and the symbols ♯ (sharp) and ♭ (flat). Every 12th fret, the note cycle repeats itself. Five note names can be called two different names. Learn both names.

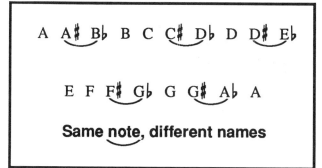

A A♯ B♭ B C C♯ D♭ D D♯ E♭

E F F♯ G♭ G G♯ A♭ A

**Same note, different names**

**Open Strings**

| Fret Numbers | E | A | D | G | B | E |
|---|---|---|---|---|---|---|
| 1 | F | A♯/B♭ | D♯/E♭ | G♯/A♭ | C | F |
| 2 | F♯/G♭ same note | B | E | A | C♯/D♭ | F♯/G♭ |
| 3 | G | C | F | A♯/B♭ | D | G |
| 4 | G♯/A♭ | C♯/D♭ | F♯/G♭ | B | D♯/E♭ | G♯/A♭ |
| 5 | A | D | G | C | E | A |
| 6 | A♯/B♭ | D♯/E♭ | G♯/A♭ | C♯/D♭ | F | A♯/B♭ |
| 7 | B | E | A | D | F♯/G♭ | B |
| 8 | C | F | A♯/B♭ | D♯/E♭ | G | C |
| 9 | C♯/D♭ | F♯/G♭ | B | E | G♯/A♭ | C♯/D♭ |
| 10 | D | G | C | F | A | D |
| 11 | D♯/E♭ | G♯/A♭ | C♯/D♭ | F♯/G♭ | A♯/B♭ | D♯/E♭ |
| 12 | E | A | D | G | B | E |
| 13 | F | A♯/B♭ | D♯/E♭ | G♯/A♭ | C | F |
| 14 | F♯/G♭ | B | E | A | C♯/D♭ | F♯/G♭ |
| 15 | G | C | F | A♯/B♭ | D | G |
| 16 | G♯/A♭ | C♯/D♭ | F♯/G♭ | B | D♯/E♭ | G♯/A♭ |
| 17 | A | D | G | C | E | A |
| 18 | A♯/B♭ | D♯/E♭ | G♯/A♭ | C♯/D♭ | F | A♯/B♭ |
| 19 | B | E | A | D | F♯/G♭ | B |
| 20 | C | F | A♯/B♭ | D♯/E♭ | G | C |
| 21 | C♯/D♭ | F♯/G♭ | B | E | G♯/A♭ | C♯/D♭ |
| 22 | D | G | C | F | A | D |

Everybody's Music Teacher